IT'S IN YOUR DNA! WHAT IS DNA?

BIOLOGY BOOK 6TH GRADE
Children's Biology Books

BABY PROFESSOR
EDUCATION KIDS

Speedy Publishing LLC
40 E. Main St. #1156
Newark, DE 19711
www.speedypublishing.com

Copyright © 2017

All Rights reserved. No part of this book may be reproduced or used in any way or form or by any means whether electronic or mechanical, this means that you cannot record or photocopy any material ideas or tips that are provided in this book.

We know that you may have heard the term "DNA" from reading books or watching television crime shows. DNA is actually the essential molecule for life and acts similar to a recipe containing instructions that instruct our body as to how to function and develop. In this book, we are going to learn more about DNA and how it knows what to do.

WHAT IS IT?

DNA stands for **Deoxyribonucleic Acid** and is a thin long molecule made of nucleotides. There are four different types of nucleotides and they are typically represented by their first letter (shown here in parenthesis): **Adenine (A), Thymine (T), Cytosine (C)** and **Guanine (G)**. They are held together by a backbone consisting of deoxyribose and phosphate, and are often referred to as the *"bases"*.

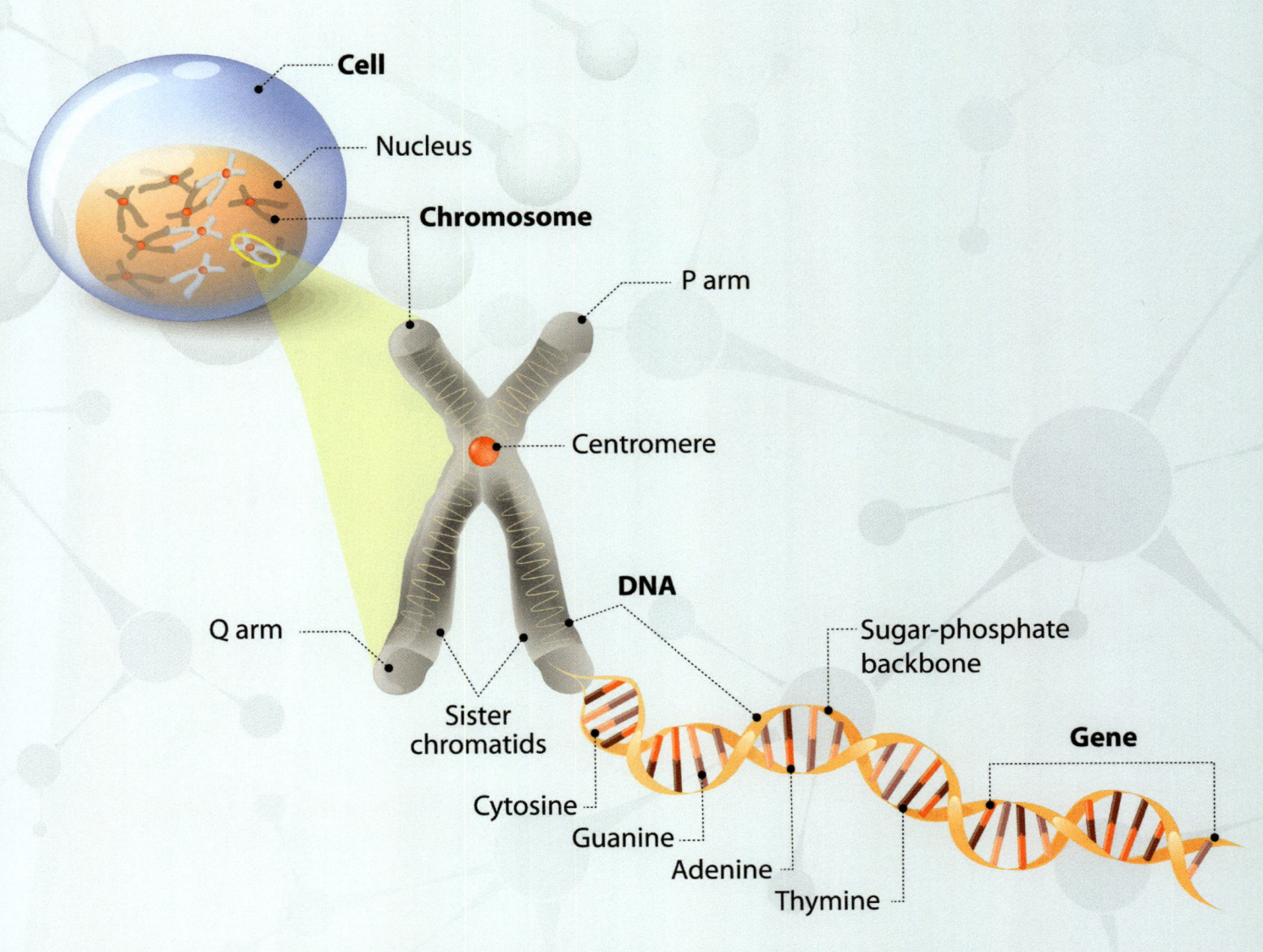

The DNA molecule is a double helix.

DNA structure

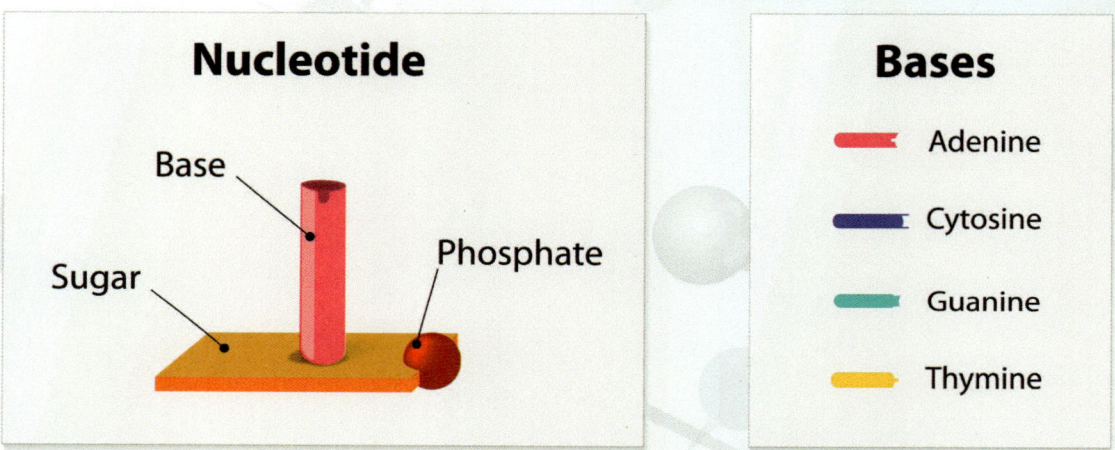
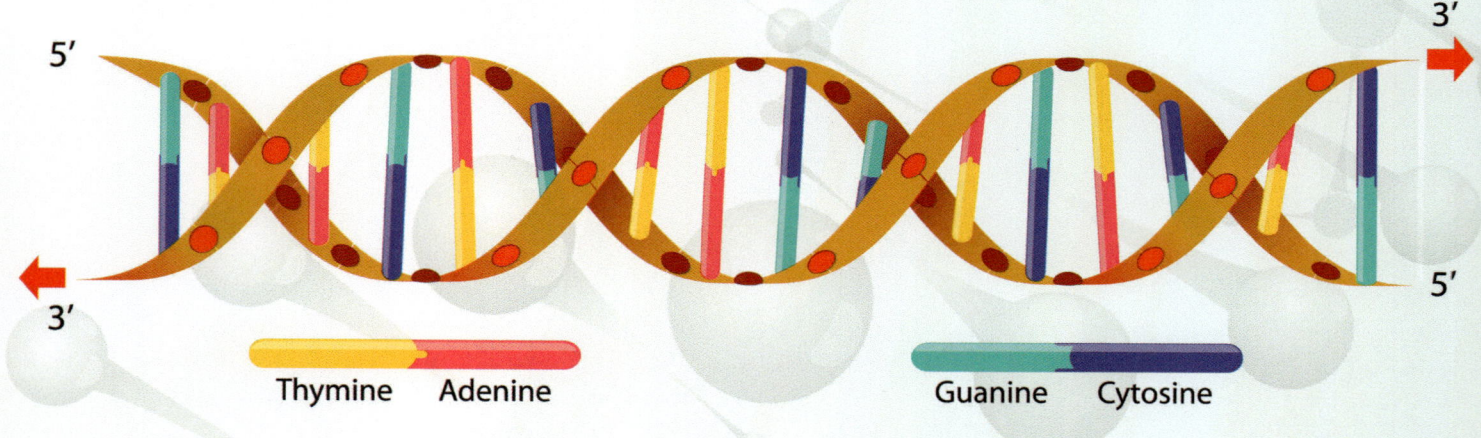

DIFFERENT CELLS IN OUR BODY

Our body consists of approximately 210 different cells and each one performs a different job in order to assist our bodily functions. There are bone cells, blood cells, and cells that make up our muscles.

DNA structure: Nucleotide, Phosphate, Sugar, and bases (thymine, adenine, guanine, and cytosine).

HOW DO OUR CELLS KNOW WHAT TO DO?

Cells obtain instructions from our DNA, which acts similar to a computer program. The cell acts like the computer or hardware, and the DNA is the code or program.

DNA and RNA.

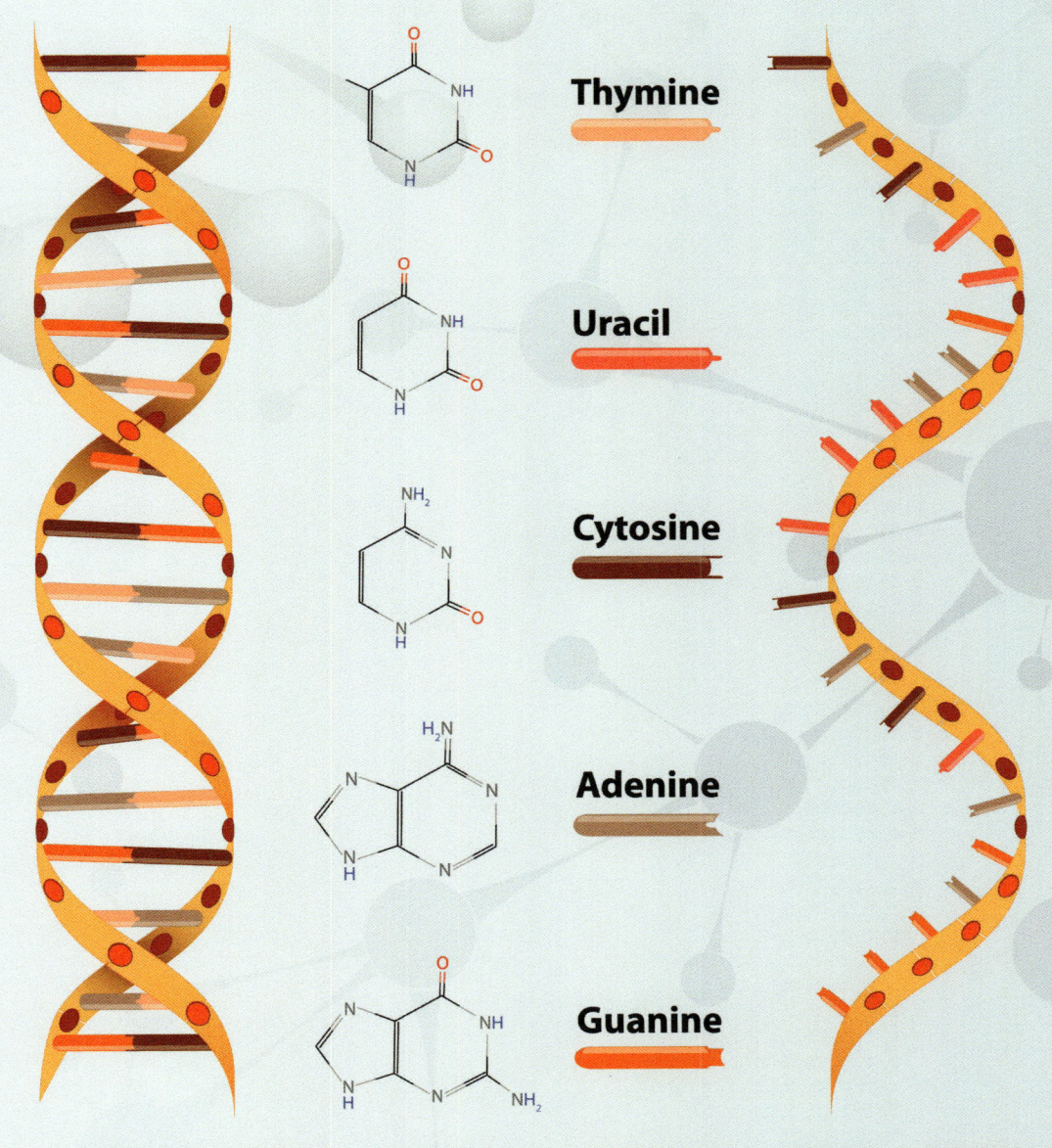

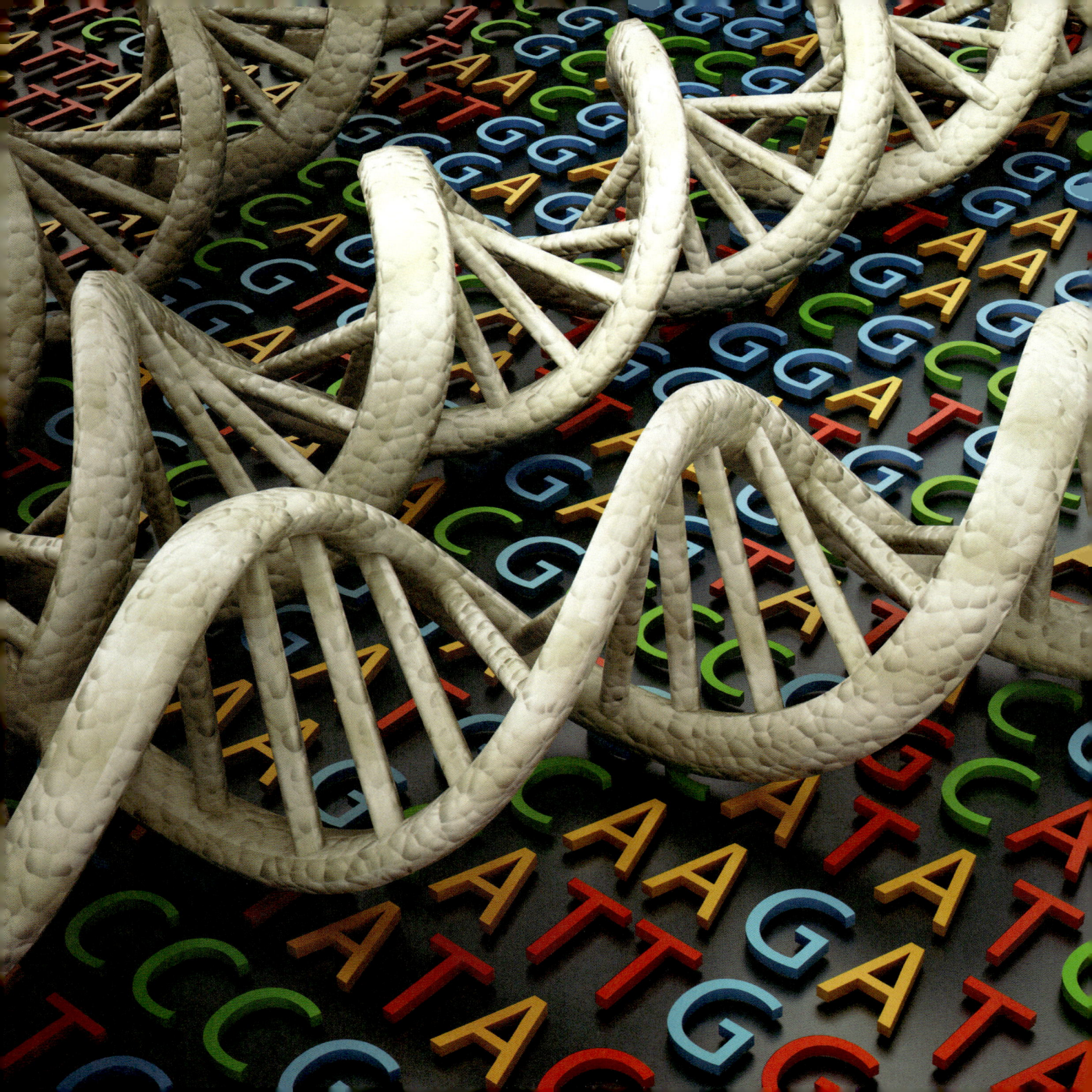

THE CODE

Our DNA code is maintained by the various letters of nucleotides, and when the cell *"reads"* the DNA instructions, each letter represents certain instructions. Every three letters create a word known as a codon.

Genetic code.

A codon string may appear similar to this: ATC TGA GGA AAT GAC CAG. While there may be only four different letters, our DNA molecules consist of thousands of letters, which allows for over a billion various combinations.

Telomere is a region of repetitive nucleotide sequences at the ends of a chromosome.

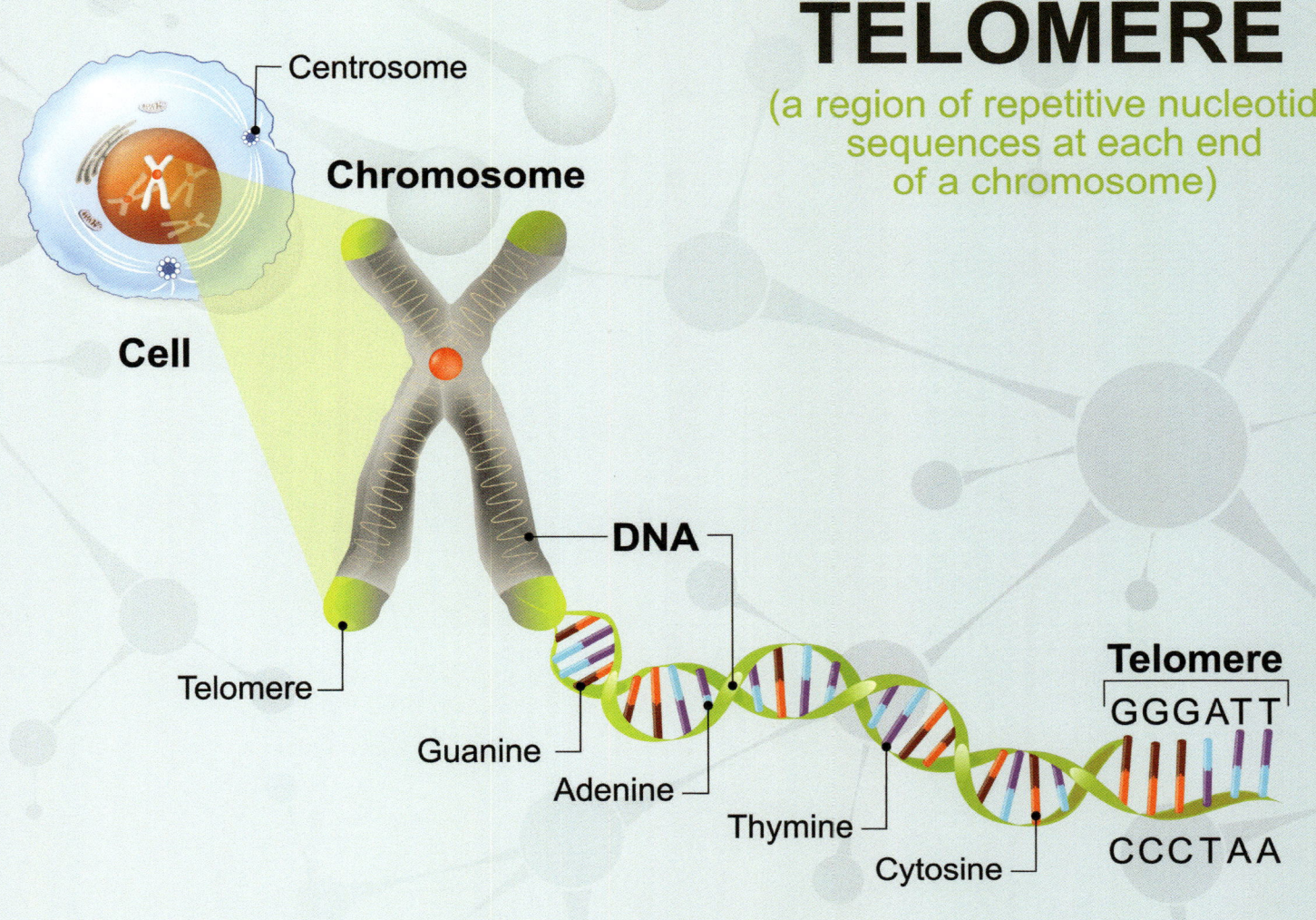

GENES

Inside each DNA string is a set of instructions that are known as genes, and these genes instruct the cell about how to create a specific protein which the cell uses in performing specific functions, in order to grow and survive.

DNA molecules.

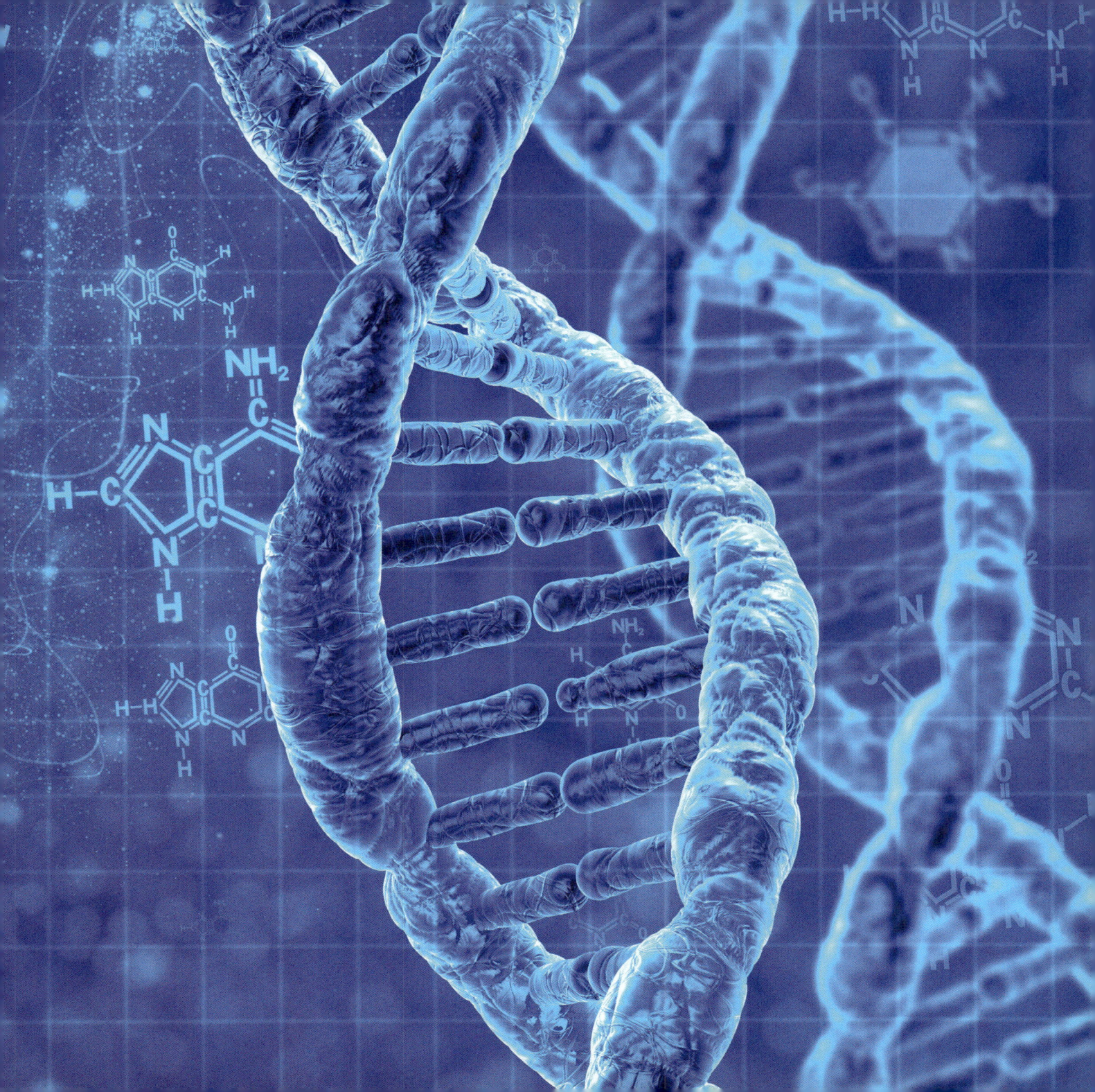

DNA MOLECULE SHAPE

Even though DNA appears to be a very thin, long strip when looked at through a microscope, DNA has a precise shape, which is known as a double helix. The backbone, which is located outside of the double helix, is what holds the DNA together, and there are two sets of backbones twisting together.

DNA replication.

DNA replication

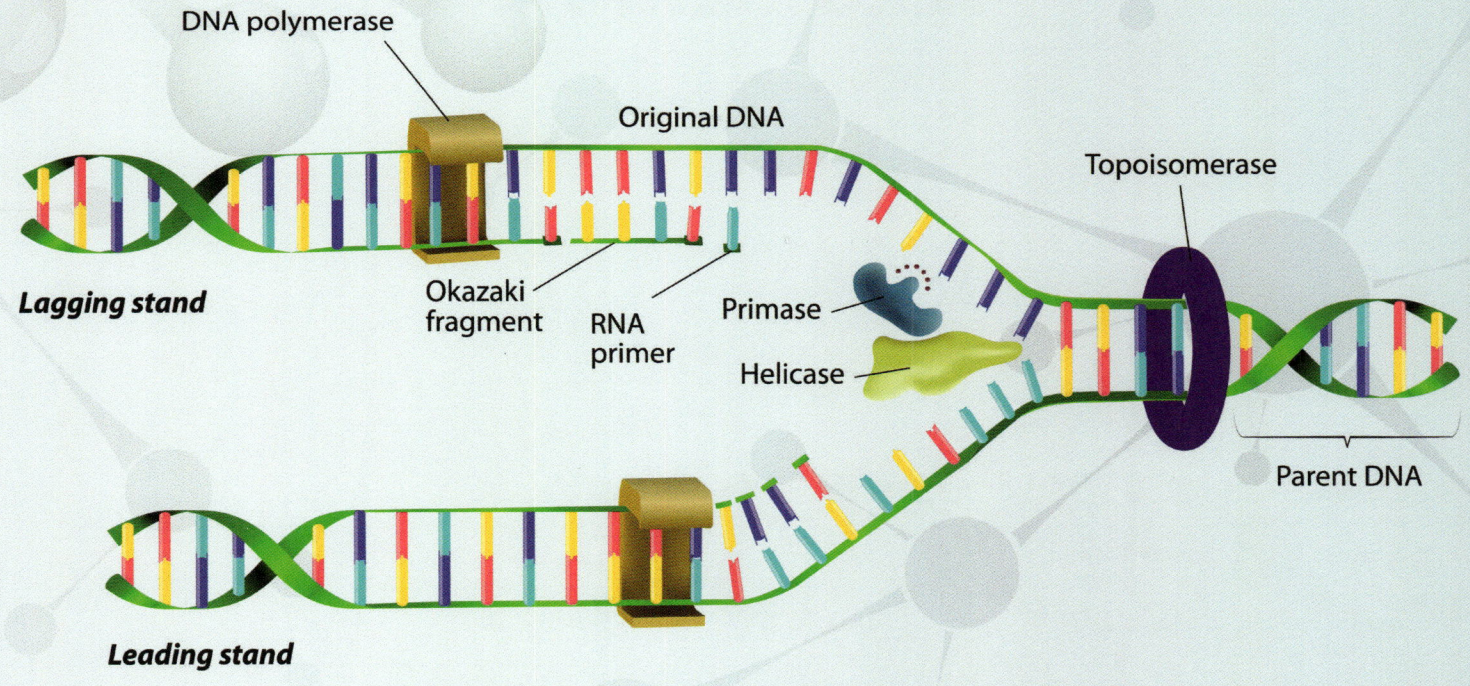

TELOMERASE

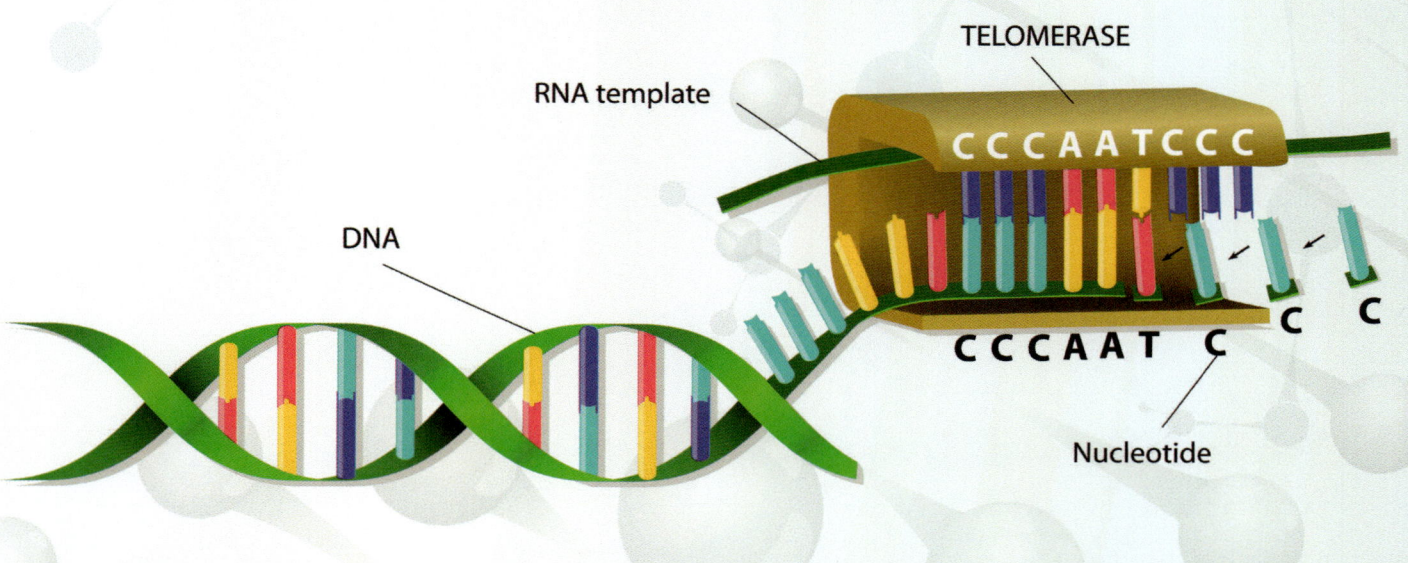

Between these two series of backbones are the nucleotides and they are represented by the letters of A, T, C and G (as we discussed earlier). A separate nucleotide connects to each of the backbones and it then connects to another nucleotide located in the center.

Telomerase is an enzyme that lengthens telomeres by adding on repeating sequences of DNA.

JAMES WATSON AND FRANCIS CRICK

James Watson and Francis Crick are known for their discovery regarding DNA structure.

Watson went to Cambridge, England in 1951 so he could work at the Cavendish Laboratory and study DNA structure. It was there he met Francis Crick, another scientist, and they soon realized that they had similar interests and started working together.

James Dewey Watson.

Maclyn McCarty with Francis Crick and James D Watson.

They went on to publish the DNA molecule structure in 1953. This discovery came to be known as one of the greatest scientific discoveries of the 20th century.

In 1962, along with Francis Crick, Maurice Wilkins, and Rosalind Franklin, Watson was awarded with the Nobel Prize in Physiology or Medicine for discovering the DNA structure. Watson continued with his genetics research, writing many textbooks, including **The Double Helix**, the bestselling book chronicling this famous discovery.

He would later serve as director of the Cold Spring Harbor Lab located in New York, and led groundbreaking cancer research. In addition, he assisted in forming the Human Genome Project mapping the human genetic sequence.

Rosalind Franklin

Franklin's notes from 1953, evaluating her X-ray diffraction data in the light of Crick and Watson's model

Francis Harry Compton Crick

FRANCIS CRICK

Francis was born on June 8, 1916 in Weston Favell, England. While his father was a shoemaker, Crick soon realized his love for science and learning and he did well in school and went on to attend the University College London. He had already won many awards for his research when he met James Watson at the Cavendish Laboratory and in 1953 made their infamous DNA double helix discovery.

After this discovery and being awarded the Nobel Prize in 1962, he continued his genetic research at Cambridge and would later work at the Salk Institute in California for several years as a research professor. Crick later died on July 28, 2004, from colon cancer.

Photograph of Francis Crick at a dinner at the Nobel Prize Winners Conference in Lindau, Germany.

DISCOVERY OF THE STRUCTURE OF DNA

While scientists had learned quite a bit about genetics in the early 1950s, they still were not able to comprehend the DNA molecule structure. To be able to understand genetics fully, they had to understand the DNA structure.

Maurice Wilkes (right) with the Meccano differential analyser in the Cambridge University Mathematics Laboratory, c1937.

The Cavendish Laboratory had created a team to answer this question before the American team headed by the well-known biochemist Linus Pauling was able to, and it soon became a race to see who would be able to be the first to figure it out.

Once they met at Cambridge, Crick and Watson soon realized their same passion for solving the DNA structure question, and that they had similar ideas as to how this question could be answered.

Linus Pauling with rope.

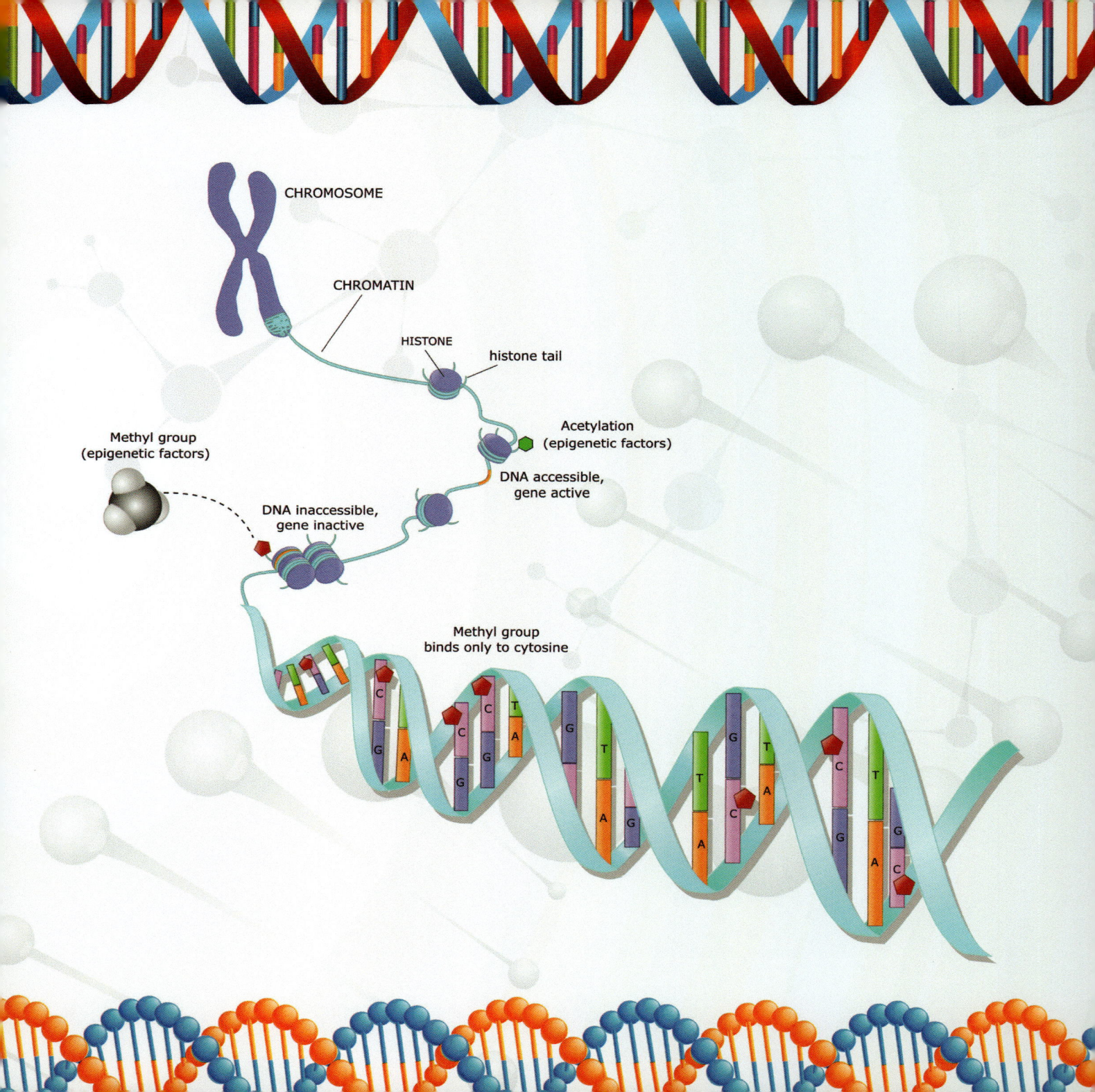

Even though their personalities were quite different, they respected one another's work and became good friends.

With the use of stick-and-ball models, they were able to test their ideas about how the DNA molecule would fit together. The first attempt failed in 1951, but they kept investigating, including the use of x-rays to get ideas for the DNA structure.

Epigenetic mechanisms: The methylation or acetylation of the DNA can activate or not the gene transcription.

Maurice Wilkins and Rosalind Franklin were the two other scientists they were working with and were experts at taking the x-ray pictures. Watson and Crick were then able to obtain some valuable information from studying the pictures taken by Wilkins and Franklin.

Comparative DNA analysis.

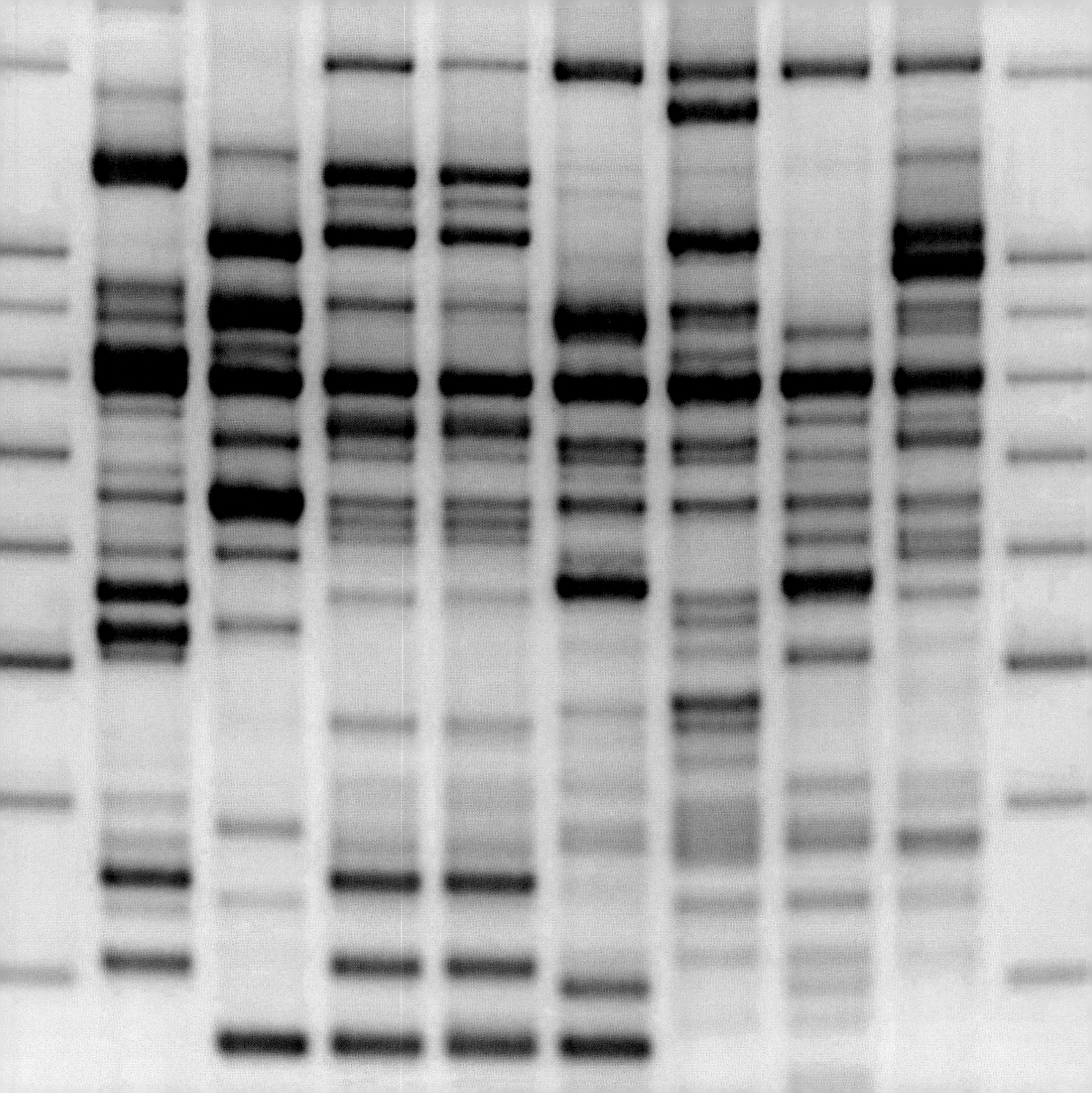

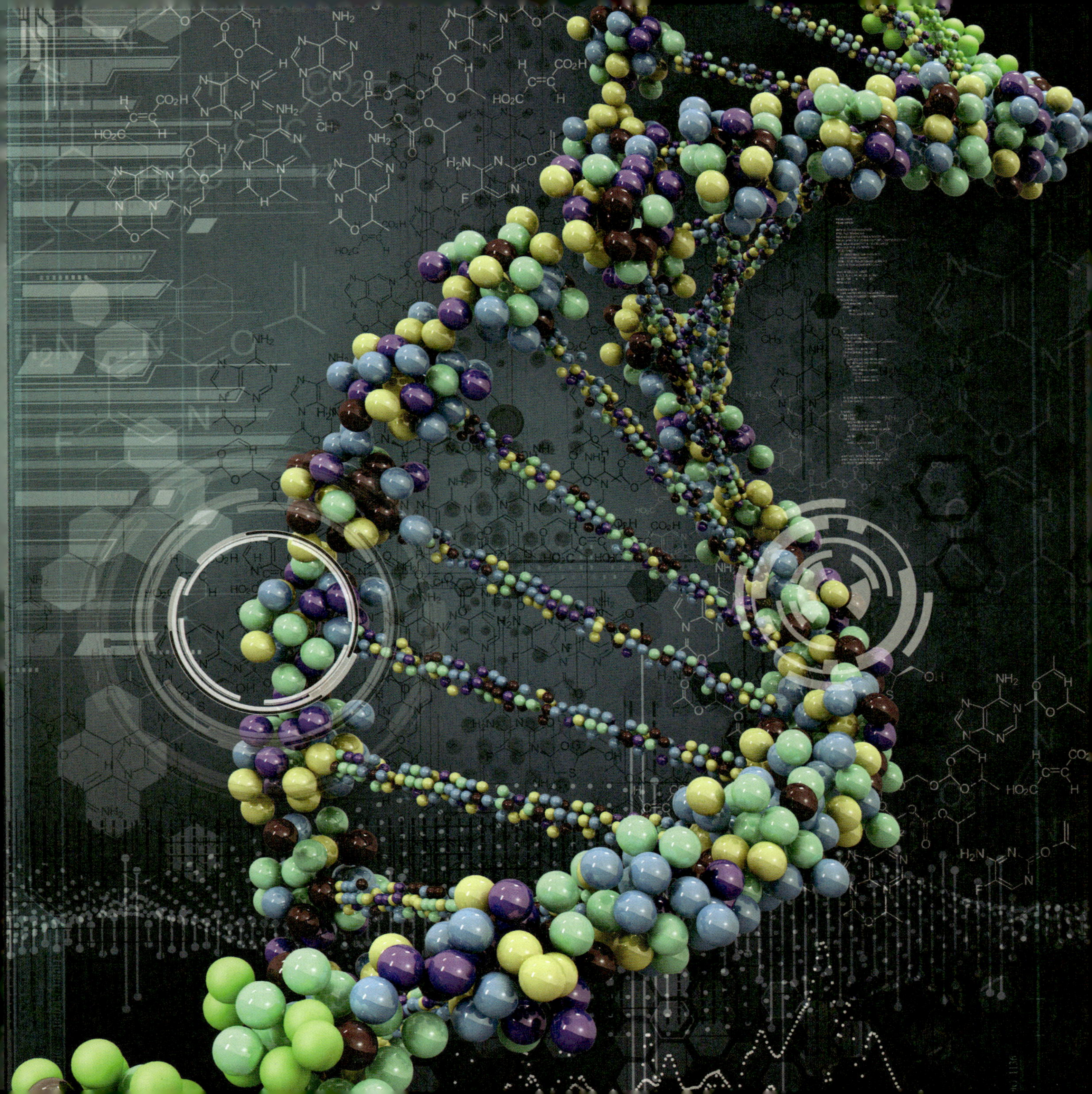

Watson and Crick were finally able to put an accurate model of DNA structure together in 1953. This model used a *"double helix"* twisting shape and would later prove to assist scientists around the world to learn about genetics.

DNA helix.

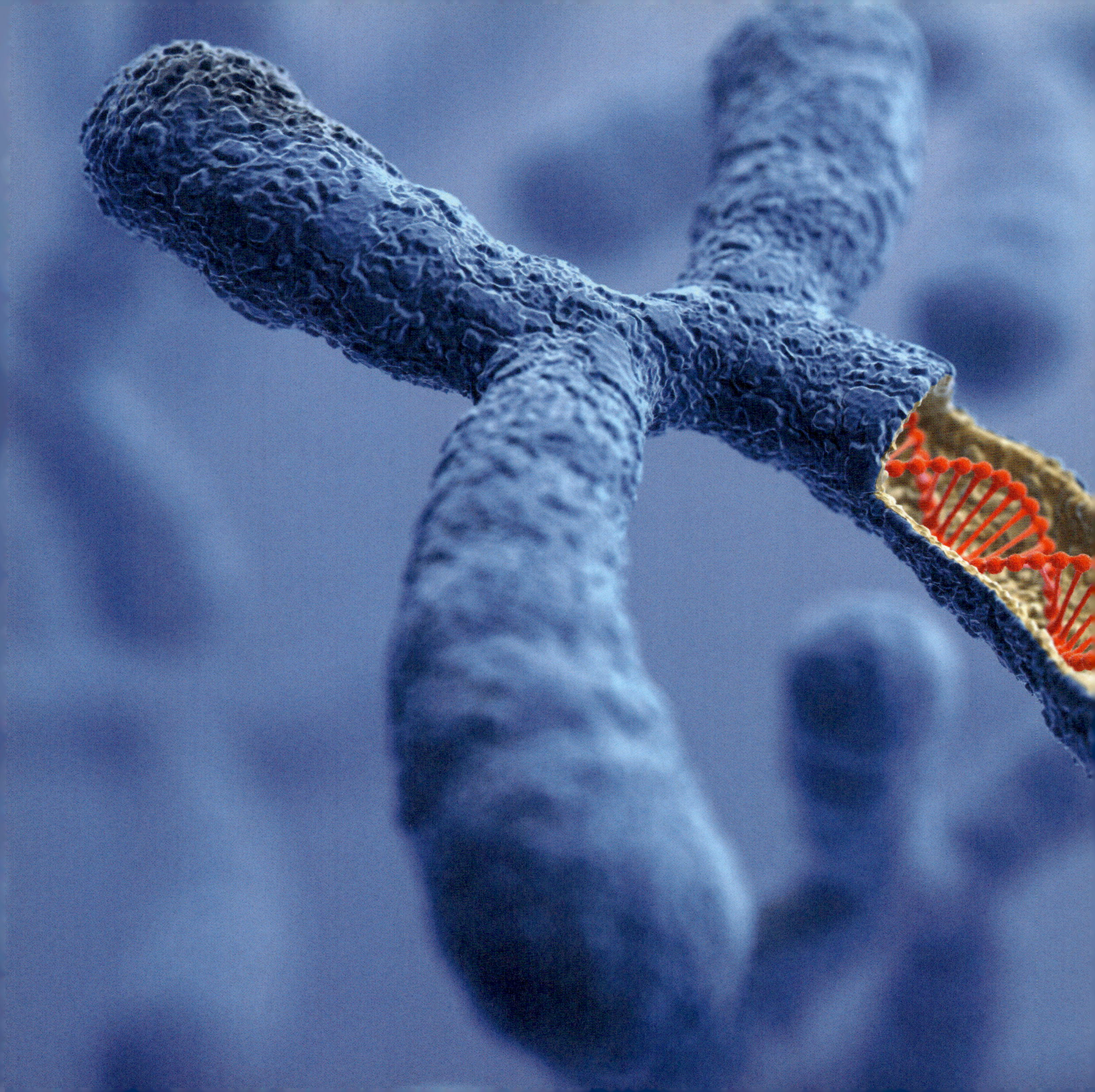

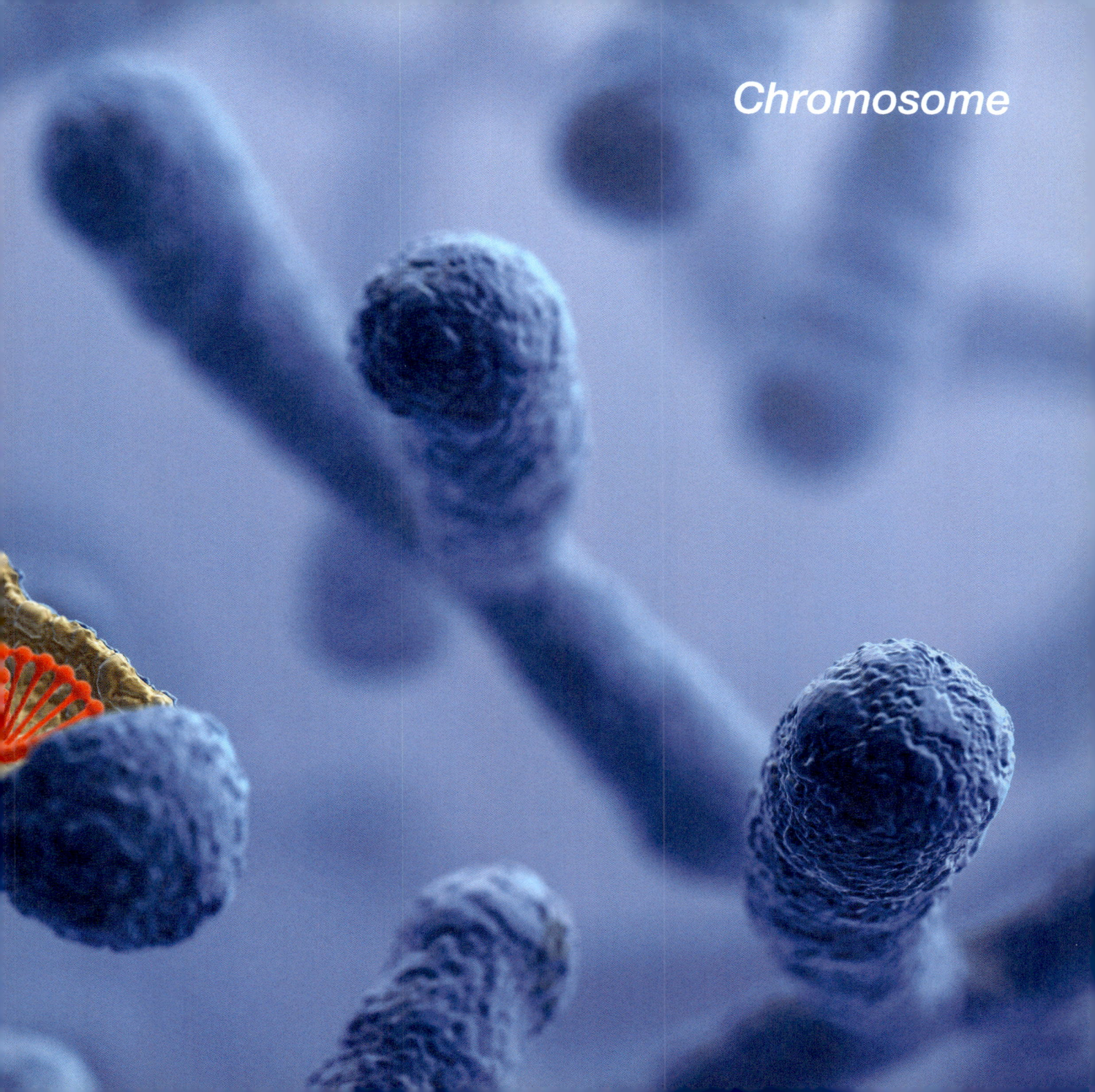

Chromosome

WHAT ARE CHROMOSOMES?

Chromosomes are very small structures that live inside cells and are made from DNA and protein. Inside the chromosomes is information that acts similar to a recipe and instructs the cells as to how to function and replicate. Each life form has a unique set of instructions. Your chromosomes decide what color your eyes are, how tall you might be, whether you are a girl or a boy.

Chromosome structure

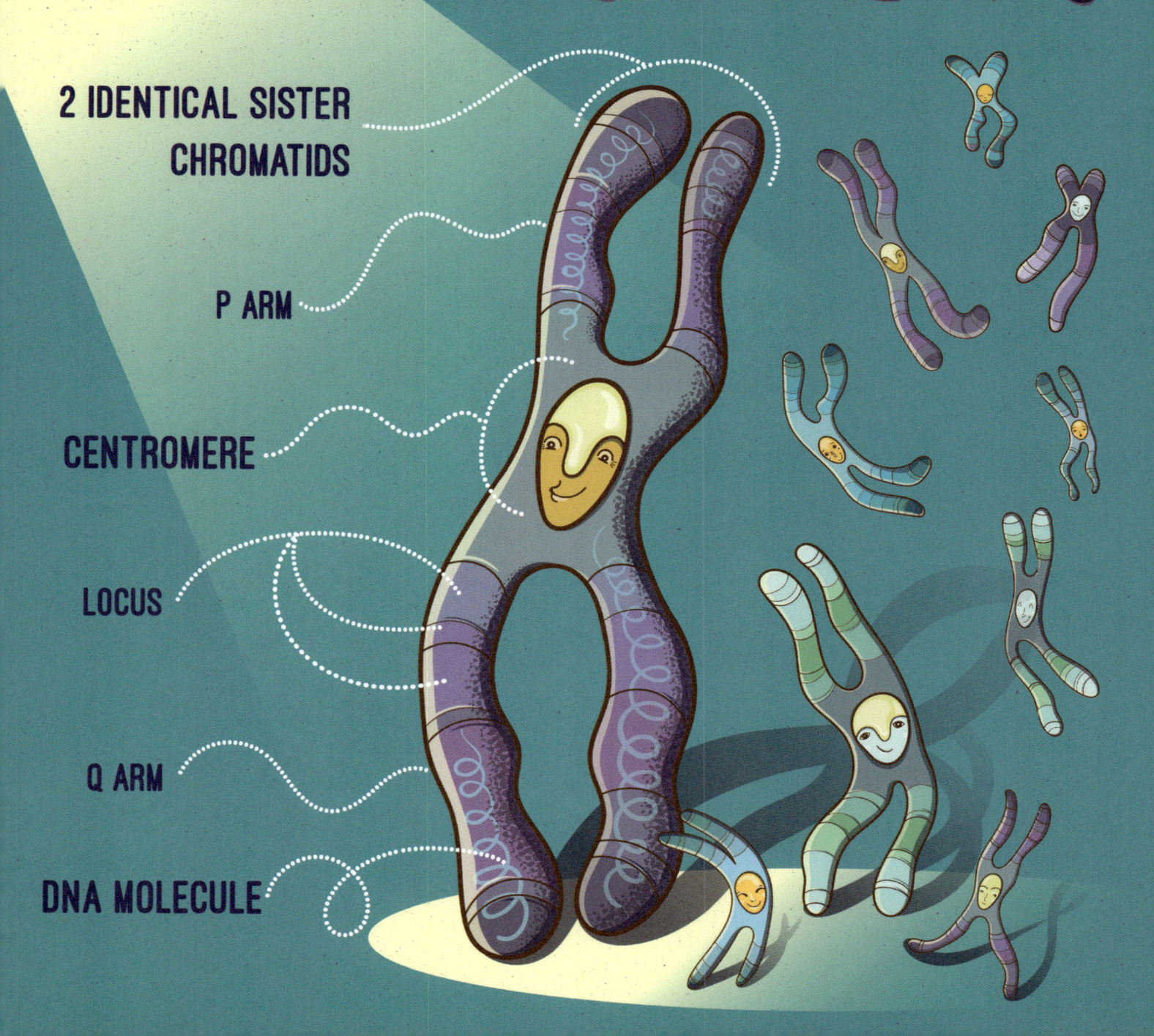

- 2 IDENTICAL SISTER CHROMATIDS
- P ARM
- CENTROMERE
- LOCUS
- Q ARM
- DNA MOLECULE

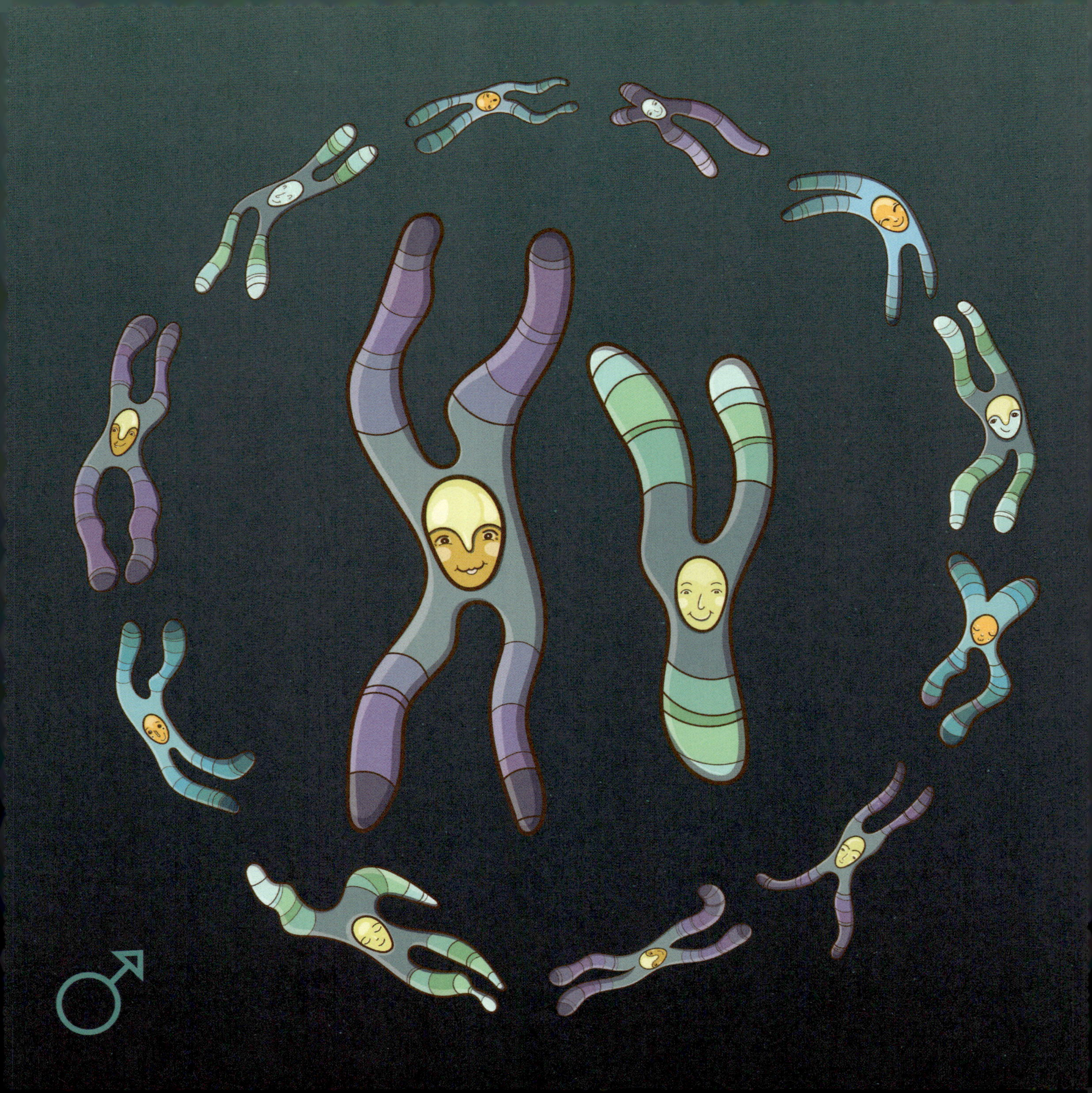

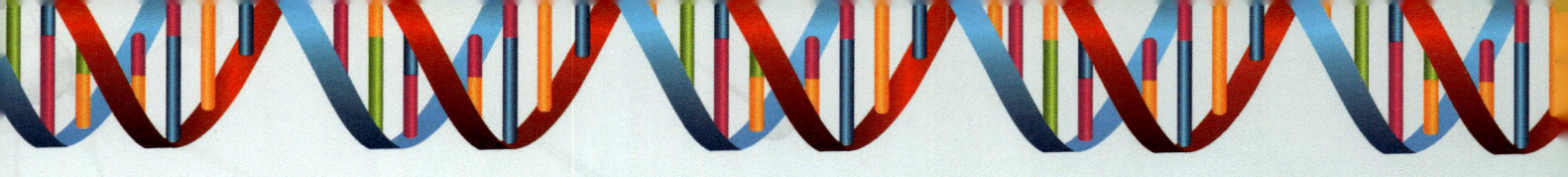

The nucleus of each cell contains chromosomes and different life forms contain a different amount of chromosomes in each cell. As humans, we have 23 pairs of chromosomes which total 46 chromosomes in each cell.

Male genotype.

ARE THEY VISIBLE TO THE HUMAN EYE?

Typically, we cannot see chromosomes. They are not even visible using a powerful microscope since they are so tiny and thin. When a cell is ready to divide, however, the chromosomes wind themselves up and become packed very tight. Using a high-power microscope, scientists are able to see chromosomes. Typically, they are in pairs and appear like little short worms.

Female genotype.

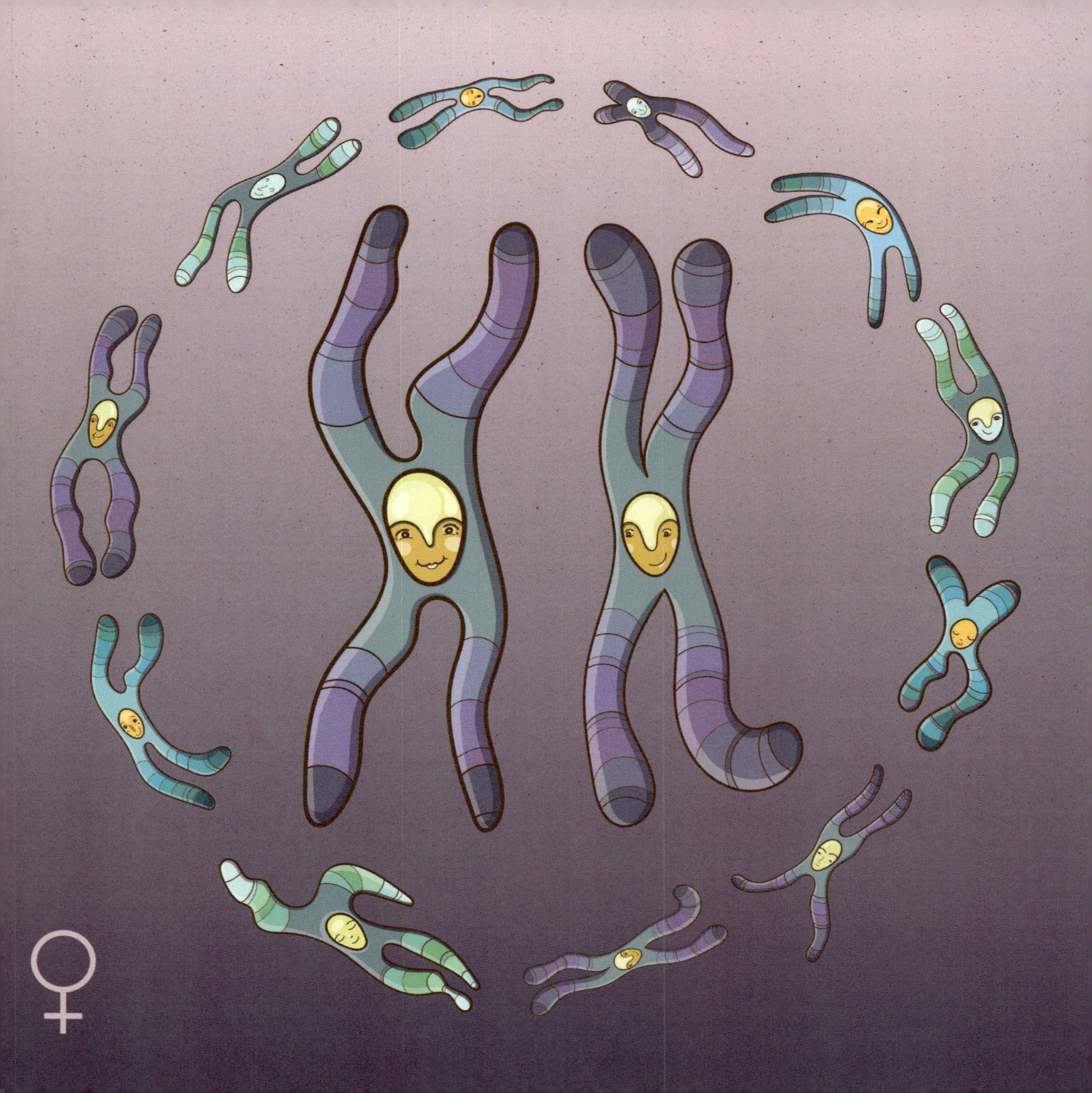

Mitosis

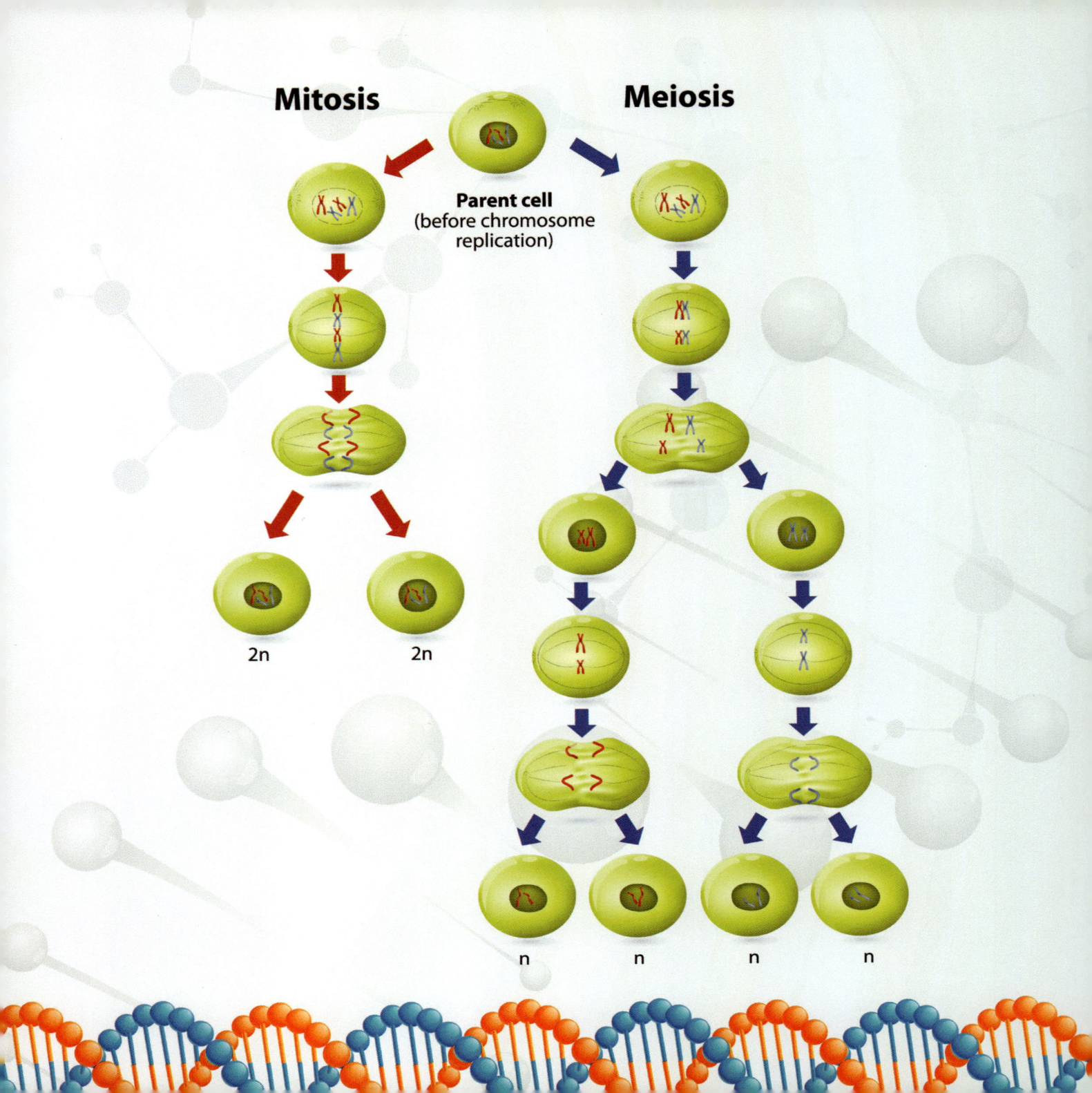

Meiosis

Parent cell
(before chromosome replication)

2n   2n

n   n   n   n

If a cell is not in the dividing process *(known as the interphase cycle of the cell)*, the chromosome is now in the chromatin form and appears as a very thin, long, strand. As the cell starts to divide, the stand duplicates itself and then winds up into tubes that are shorter. Prior to the split, the two tubes are pinched together to a point known as the centromere. The tubes' shorter arms are known as the **"P arms"** and the arms that are longer are known as the **"Q arms"**.

Meiosis and Mitosis. Mitosis is the process of asexual reproduction. Meiosis is sexual reproduction with two pairs of genes.

DIFFERENT CHROMOSOMES

Each chromosome carries different information, such as one may carry information about height and eye color and another one might determine your blood type.

Chromosome

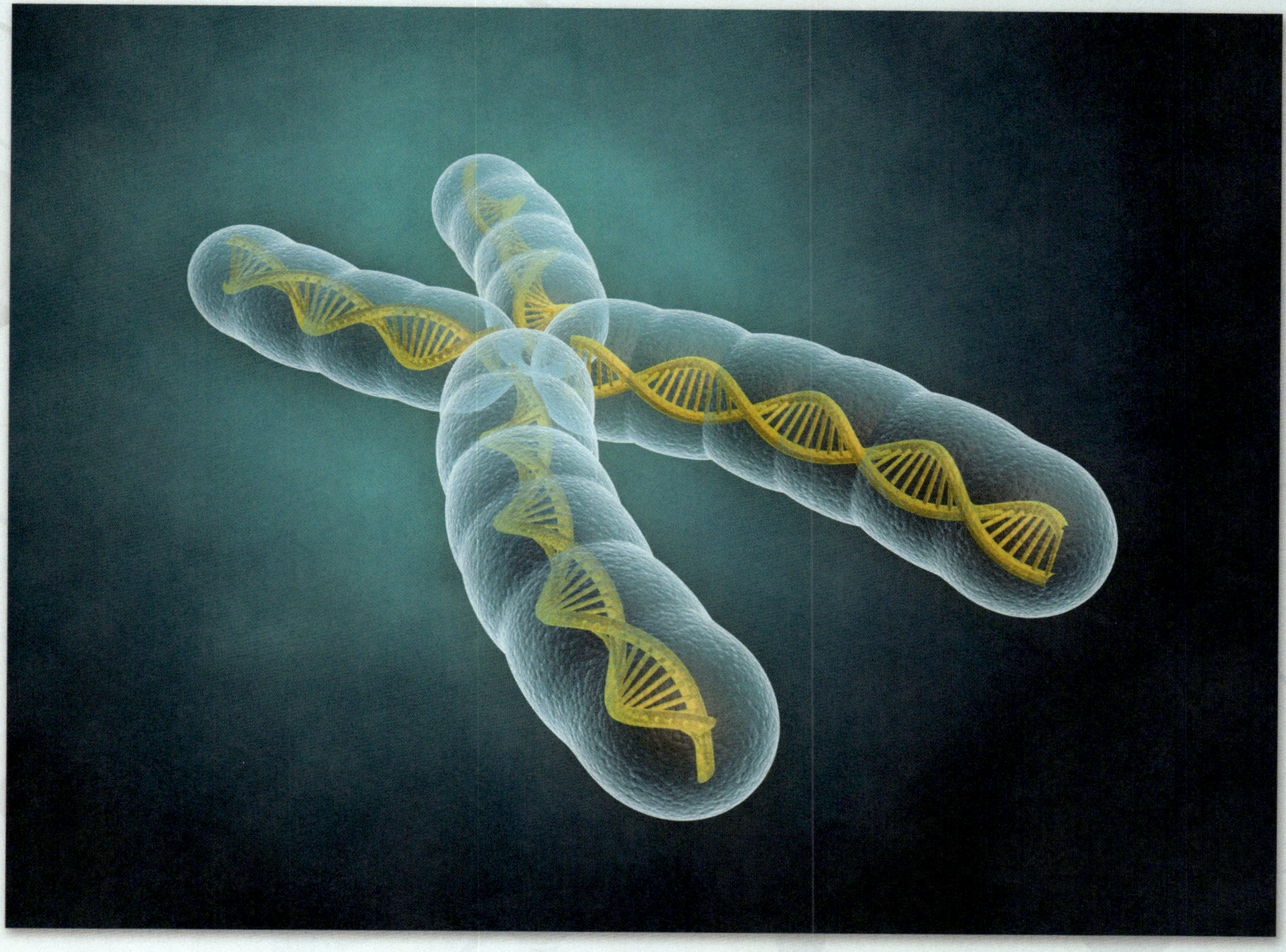

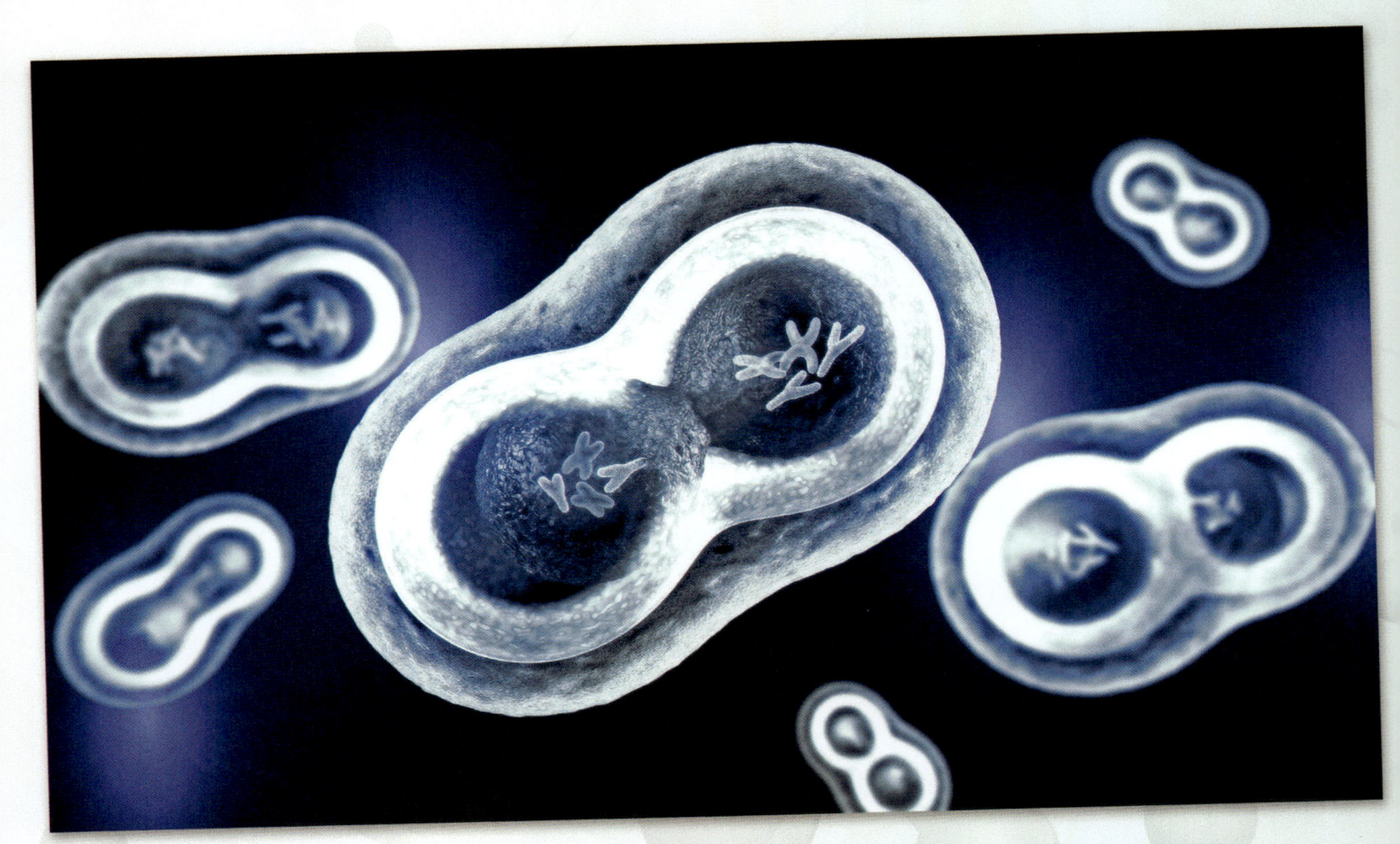

Transparent cells with nucleus, cell membrane and visible chromosomes

GENES

Every chromosome contains specific sections of DNA known as genes, and each one contains the recipe or code for making a certain protein. These proteins then determine what traits we inherit from our parents as well as determining how we grow. This gene is often referred to as a unit of heredity.

ALLELES

When referencing a gene, we are talking about a part of DNA. The gene determining your eye color would be a perfect example. When referencing a certain sequence of the gene *(similar to the sequence that gives you blonde hair as opposed to the sequence that gives you brown hair),* this is known as an allele. Everyone has a gene determining the color of their hair, however, only brunettes have the allele making their hair brown.

Eye color

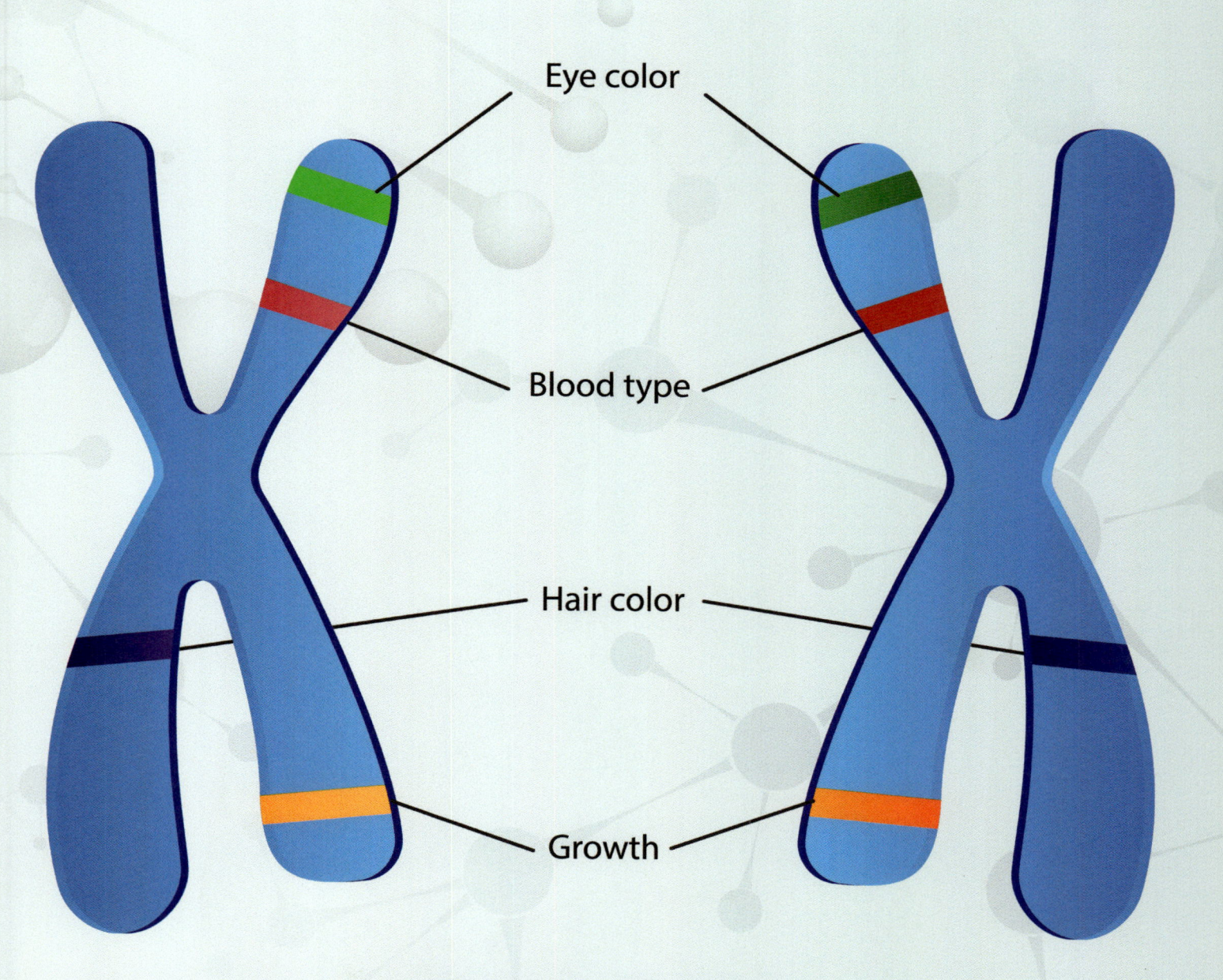

Blood type

Hair color

Growth

Genes and Alleles

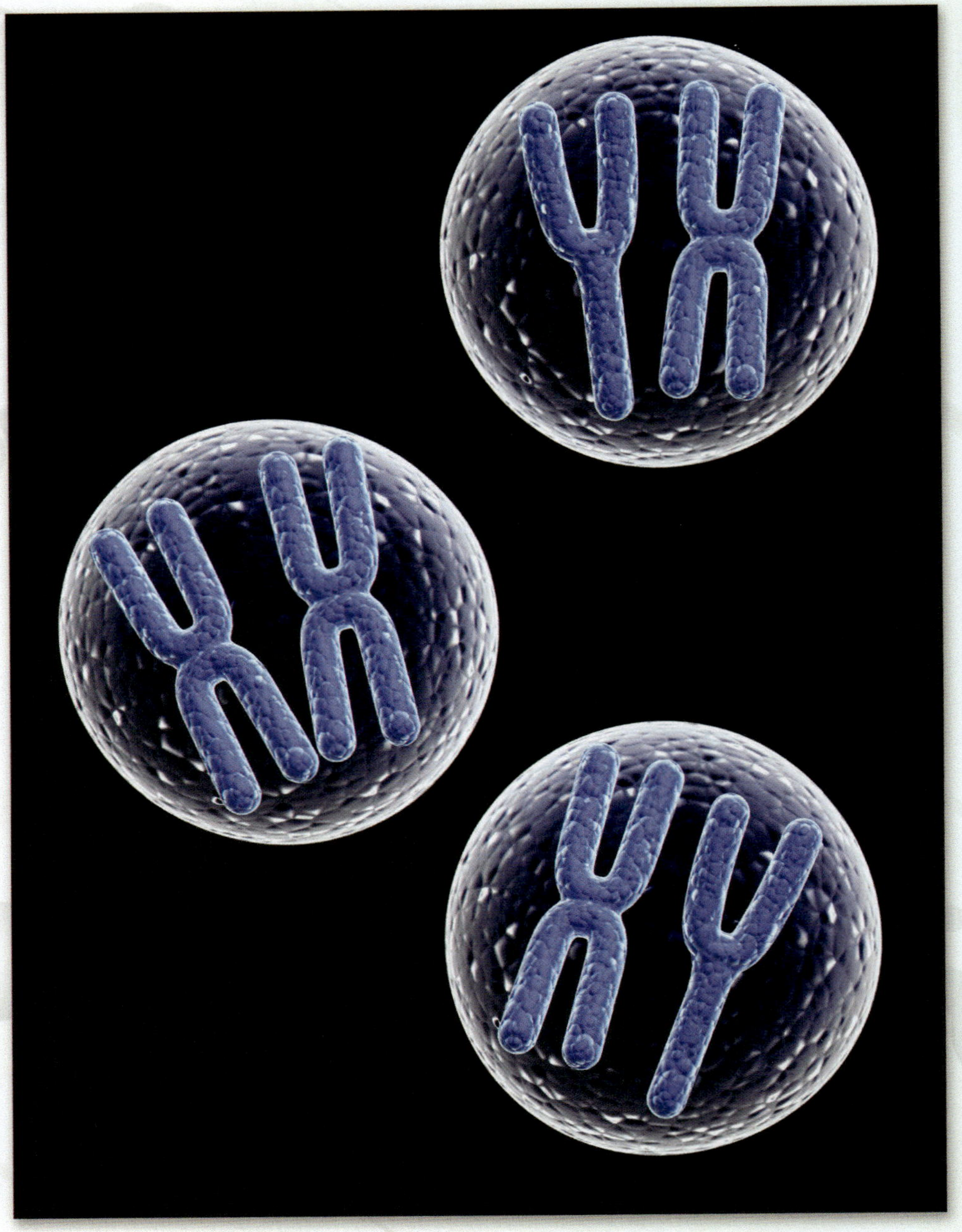

THE HUMAN CHROMOSOMES

As discussed earlier, as humans we have 23 pairs of chromosomes which totals 46 chromosomes. We obtain 23 chromosomes from our father and 23 chromosomes from our mother. These pairs are numbered by scientists from 1 to 22 and there is then the extra pair known as the "X/Y" pair. This pair determines whether you are a girl or a boy. The boys have one X and one Y chromosome, known as the **XY**, and girls have two X chromosomes referred to as the **XX**.

X and Y chromosomes in cell.

CHROMOSOMES OF VARIOUS ANIMALS

Different life forms contain different numbers of chromosomes; a rabbit has 44, a horse has 64, and the fruit fly has 8 chromosomes.

The next time you are watching a criminal television show and you hear the term "DNA", you will be able to know what they are referring to and how they use it to solve crimes.

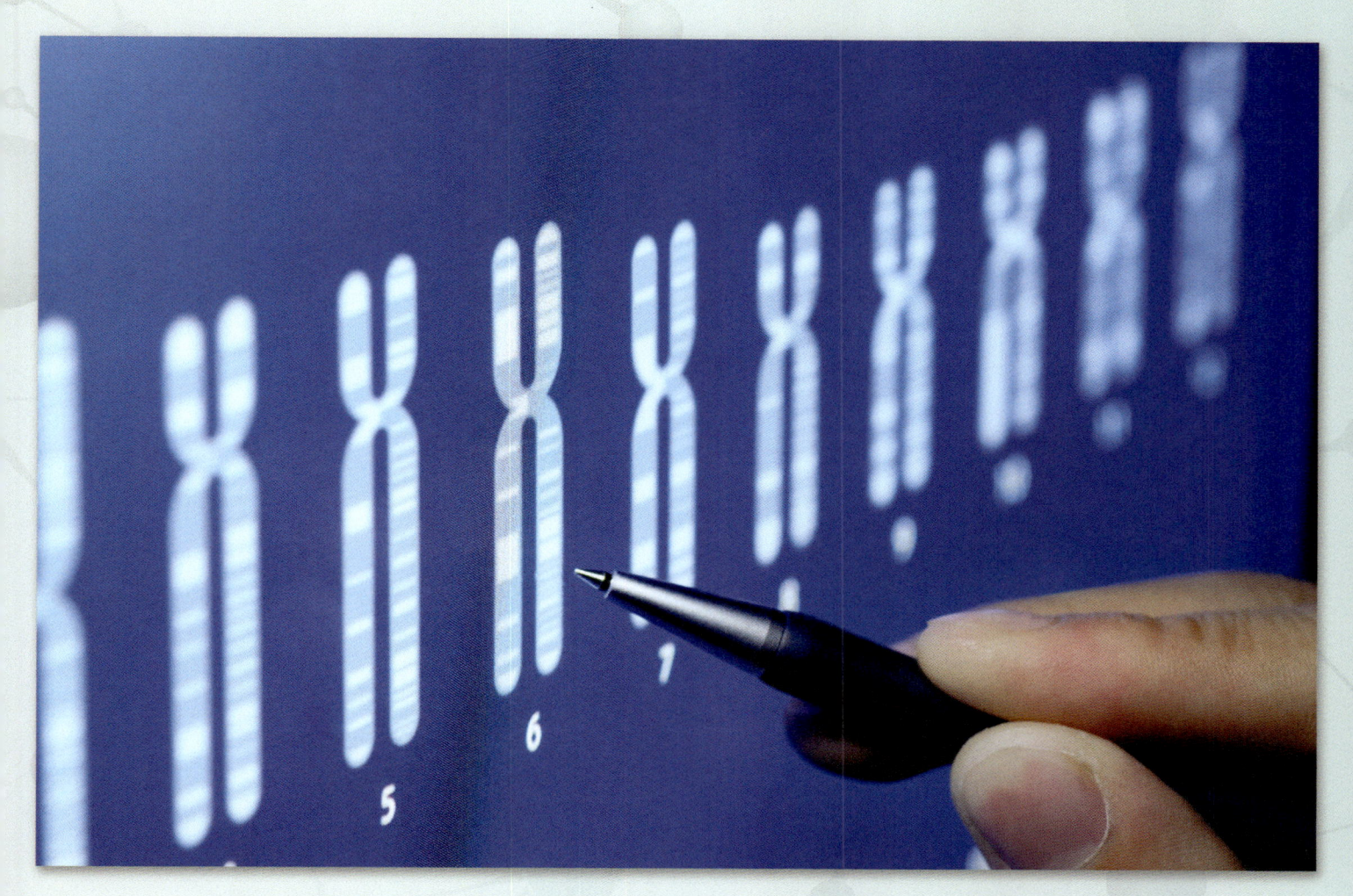

Scientific research and study on chromosomes.

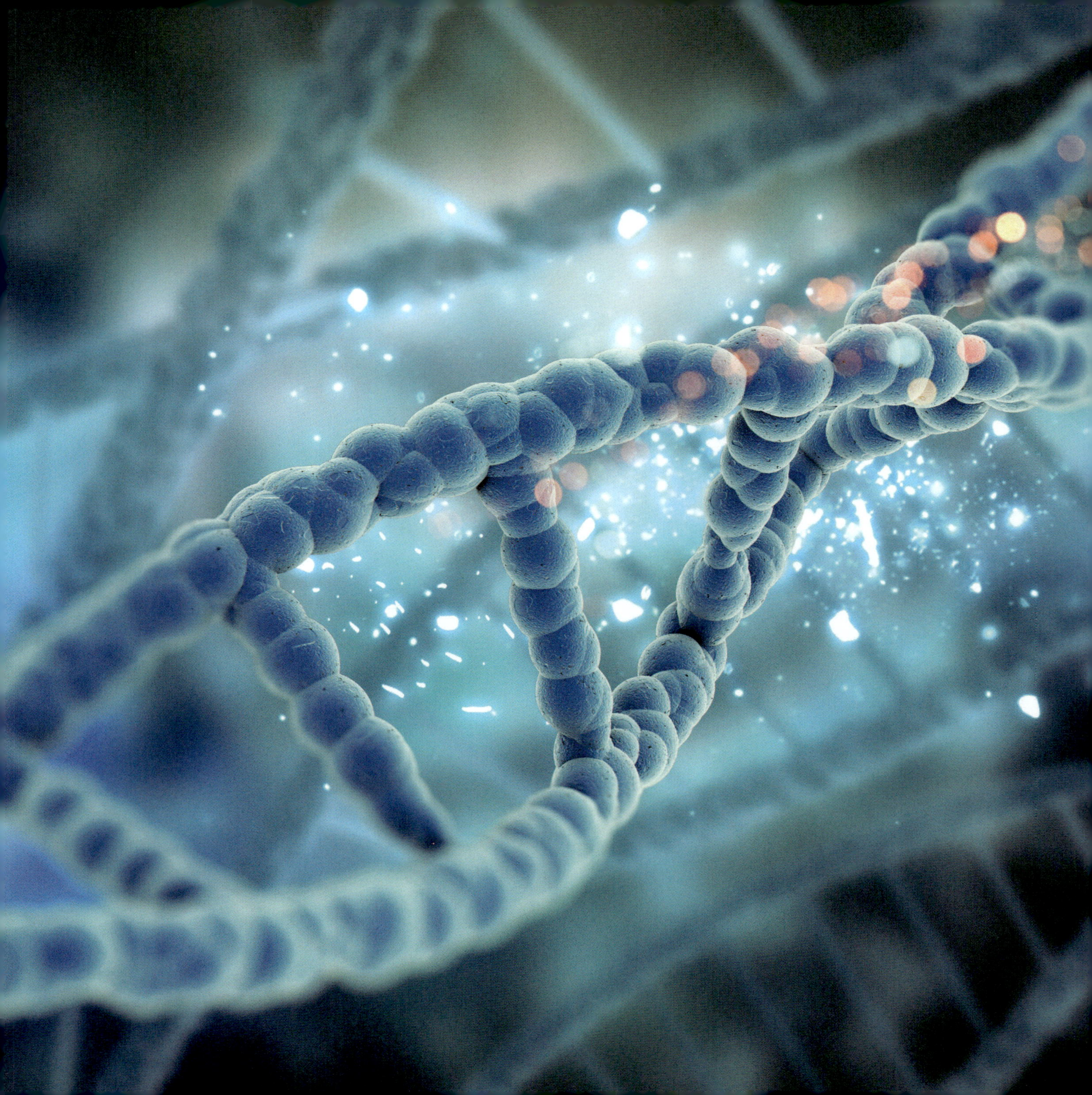

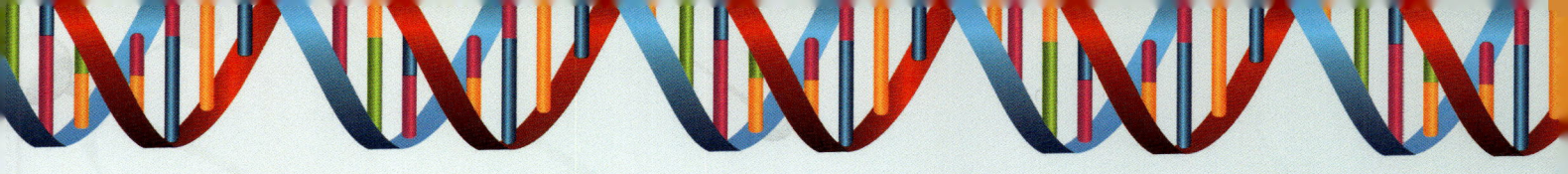

To learn about DNA, genetics, and chromosomes, you can go to your local library, research the internet, and ask questions of your teachers, family and friends.

DNA double helix molecules and chromosomes.

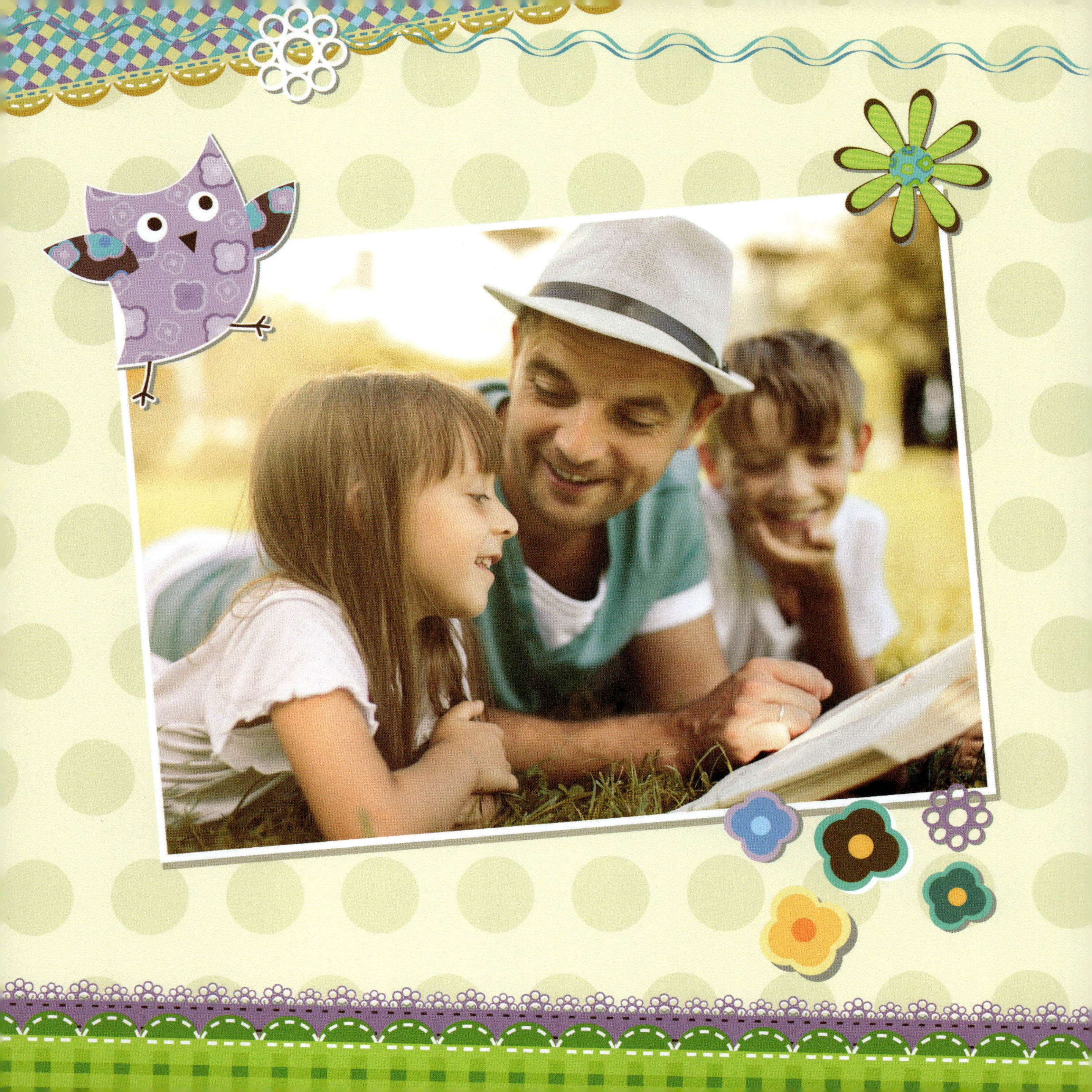

Visit

BABY PROFESSOR
EDUCATION KIDS

www.BabyProfessorBooks.com

to download Free Baby Professor eBooks and view our catalog of new and exciting Children's Books

Printed in Great Britain
by Amazon